How to Create a Turnaround in Your Organization?

By

Chakrapani Srinivasa

How to Create a Turnaround in Your Organization?

by Chakrapani Srinivasa

Dedicated to My Dear Parents

Preface

The new era presents new realities such as borderless market places and discriminating consumers, who are unmoved by appeals to select home built products for patriotic reasons.

Consumers look for the best value.

This turnaround can be achieved if good HRD instruments and systems are practiced in flying colors.

That will lead to Quality Management.

The choice of the organization systems, structure and style ends up deeply affecting the psyche and spirit of all employees.

There's insufficient recognition that the most important system is the human system.

If the human system is powerfully shaped by the organizational roles people play, then the most effective way to change behavior therefore, is to put people into a new organizational context, which imposes new roles, responsibilities and relationships on them.

Contents

Quality Process

Change is now in the air, and quality process is on many lips.

But there's little real change. That's because, most companies now examining their processes are not extending their enquiry to their entire organization.

That's a serious omission, spurred by Japanese success and grounding problems in competitiveness; research and retrospective analysis have provided increasingly compelling evidence of the need for a change.

This change could be brought out by various HRD instruments and subsystems.

Used in any organizational setup, each has a specific purpose and power to build a nation to a mighty force to face the competing world.

Various HRD Instruments and Sub Systems

The new era presents new realities such as borderless market places and discriminating consumers, who are unmoved by appeals to select home built products for patriotic reasons.

Consumers look for the best value.

This can be achieved if good HRD instruments and systems are practiced in flying colors.

That will lead to Quality Management.

The choice of the organization systems, structure and style ends up deeply affecting the psyche and spirit of all employees. There's insufficient recognition that the most important system is the human system.

If the human system is powerfully shaped by the organizational roles people play, then the most effective way to change behavior therefore, is to put people into a new organizational context, which imposes new roles, responsibilities and relationships on them.

HRD Instruments:
- Organizational Effectiveness Department.

- Performance Appraisal
- Review meetings, analysis counseling, knowing the reaction
- Role diagnosis
- Skills improvement techniques
- Training
- Communication practices
- Rotation of jobs'
- Enforcement of TQM techniques.

Organizational Effectiveness Department:

Instead of naming it as HRD department, the CEO of Cummins christened it as OE Dept.

"As the effectiveness is the net result I have renamed if so says the CEO".

This forms the foundation for building up HRD and upgrading the people behind us and below us.

It helps to firmly establish the character of the organization which the people should know. It is also one of the pillars of total quality management.

It aids to orient employee's focus and activity to their product as well as on their job.

"The whole country can't get better overnight. But it can start getting better right away. Each business makes its own decisions. Each can be substantially and even dramatically improved.

However, the extent of the success in each case depends on the willingness to abandon the traditional approach for a new and better way. This could be achieved by HRD section of an organization. - Aditya Vikram Birla.

The above statement clearly speaks about the importance of HRD or organizational effectiveness division.

Performance Appraisal:

The exercise was mooted to amend the promotion policy to make it totally performance oriented. But on instrument for measurement was needed to fulfill this aim. To inculcate culture and convenience people that their career growth was linked the performance of company, the performance appraisal was found to be an ideal magic wand.

"Performance appraisal shapes people's attitude so that they will always be willing to do the best work or service people" - S. Dedhia, California based Chairman of the international Chapter of the American Society for Quality control.

Knosuka Matsushita, the founder of Matsushita Electrical Industrial Company wrote an article in an issue of Peace, Happiness and Prosperity, as follows:

"Performance appraisal binds your workforce to quality. Give them a free hand. They must have the power to execute solutions and they develop.

Frontline staff must be able to re-address complaints without running for approval to the boss.

To build a quality empire "Empower"!

Performance appraisal supports

- To see that the business plans are executed to meet the annual quality goals.

- To determine how the goals, the wish lists are converted into deeds.

- To develop mindset for a change.

- To bring forth new culture to pour in new force and life to the organization.

- To enable individuals to speak out openly what they have in mind about their ability, future plans and hindrances for achieving them.

- To accommodate every individuals' views, aspirations dreams and wild or soft comments for improvements.

- To allow a blood stream full of vigor and aspirations to face the competition.

- To bring a cultural change and uplift performance appraisal and paves a flowery way.

In a press interview Mr. Joseph, M. Juran said:

"You see the school curriculum that managers attend – whether they are Engineers or Business school graduates or financial graduates – does not expose them to concept of culture, which they will discover after they get out and try to introduce to change this performance appraisal in actual people".

Review Meetings, Analysis, Counseling

Studying the reactions of the employees when something introduced new to an organization is vital step for HRD.

In Reliance, when Ambani introduced changes, then a review meeting was conducted immediately to study the reactions of their employee.

This is to establish openness says Ambani "People are great force, Trust gives trust, Giving orders and waiting or results greed will not enforce smooth operation in an organization. The top management managers should analyze the pitfalls, bad or good consequences and accommodate accordingly.

The views of the staff, if any, should be heard. A good listener is a good business man,   -N.R. Narayanamoorthy, Chairman – Infosys.

The employee's difficulties and struggles can be solved by counseling and review meetings.

"If you allocate resources, but forget to communicate with employees – you will have on utterly ineffective TQM exercise. - Chairman WIPRO.

The main purposes of review meetings and counseling are fulfilled if they are meticulously handled. Full freedom of speech and liberty to express adverse remarks will pay well in the long run.

As said by India's CEO, we should make workers champion individual customers' requirements. A good counseling does this artistically.

On quality strategy, CEO of Indal says, "There are 3 types of resistances. There was some resistance because the whole concept was so new. With the quality movement going to the grass roots, workers have to be empowered. So, some people felt a loss of power. The third group simply didn't believe that it could be done.

We have won the first group completely and say 70% of the last group through counseling, review meetings, discussions and by showing them the results.

The second group is getting smaller as they realize the tremendous benefits from the movement.

The third group started believing after seeing the results. So, a good strategy for discussions, review analysis will fetch good successful results.

Role diagnosis

What are the roles of every individual in an organization? This is to be seen critically and diagnosed. Then only all strategies will work out smoothly and pave way for successful HRD.

'The limitations of powers to be exercised, his commitments, expectations, duties and the area over which his capabilities will extend had to be given in a point blank to individuals.

This will help him to sail smoothly in the organization without hurdles.

Duality begins from personal role'.says **Madhav Mehra**.- Quality Consultant

.

In IFB Industries, the CEO says that there are no communication barriers between managers and as the firm grew it become system oriented. They felt that they may lose personal touch. But due to perfect role diagnosis, this hurdle was overcome and IFB's strength lies in its strong entrepreneurial spirit and the excellent management / employee relations due to good diagnosis.

Who should do what? If this is earmarked clearly by the management then a good development can be seen in human resources.

IFB's periodic Works Committee meetings of staff from all departments provide the manager with feedback on the effectiveness of the Quality Systems they were introducing and cleared the workers doubts.

In addition to this is the monthly quality review meeting, which goes through process as a matter of routine and discussed targets, improvements, customer complaints possible remedies and vital hindrances.

Process audit is continuous during production with process data being recorded by the quality control department and computer system.

The moment a worker notices a non-conformance, he stops the machine and alerts quality control team. The maintenance team and quality system analysts deal together and move with people involved and diagnose the situation. Until the team comes up with an answer, the particular machine or process / system will be shutdown.

IFB's current rejection rate is only 0.25%. This credit goes to good analysis, review meetings regarding men, machine and materials.

A review of human capabilities and sound counseling can make thorough control over all non-conformities.

Throughout production, the customer is also given access to process data and feed back is encouraged.

This is the success of IFB, says it's CEO.

"It was our desire for excellence that motivated us to come up with our quality philosophy in HRD, which believes that personal quality is the key to product quality".   -
Mr. Bijon Nag -CEO IFB.

The review analysis helps to make everyone work in the same direction. No clashes, no controversies, no pessimistic approach and no pitfalls.

Skills Improvement Techniques:

"Don't start with the idea that man is bad. You should know how to touch the right cords in a worker to make him skillful. - J.R.D. TATA

Through the above statement, the most respectable businessman clearly speaks out how important it is to make an approach to make an individual / worker skillful to achieve production and desired goals.

There may be hidden skills, which may not be seen face to face. A good business can view it and tap the rich talents useful for his organization.

When Mr.Ambani, Chairman Reliance appointed a finance division head as the Managing Director of a textile division many raised their eye brows. But Ambani was calm and cool and said "I can view a potential in-built in him to make that project a successful one.

And it happened in reality. When Ambani raised the skill of that finance division individual, the magic happened.

Cost consciousness aided the project too well along with the knowledge of textile poured into his mind.

Ambani was right.

When Ambani who knew little about textile technology can be a Chairman, why not he be a M.D., said an Economic expert to the press.

Bewildering achievement took place in textile division when skills developed with confidence.

If you have the urge to be the best and perfect, nothing can stop you. But we need a mechanism to provide us with that urge. That is done by skill development exercises. It changes a man! A certain transformation does take place!

Training:

What's required in business today is not adding assets but knowing how to be more competitive with existing resources.

With liberalization, industries need to gear up for global markets.

The multinationals are here. And the customer's expectations are sky high on quality. Fighting to survive is not only necessary but imperative.

The buzzword of management gurus today is "Leverage your resources train them", they say to achieve success.

Training does magic.

It helps to deliver higher value at lower costs. The essence of high performance is the classic result of training.

It is a technology broker. It adds pep into the life of every individual. Training makes a man perfect.

Companies should invest heavily in educating their most valuable resource. This will become their competitive edge.

Self directing teams of employees professional and managers will continuously improve their own performance and drive cross-functionally quality improvement throughout the organization.

"Companies should use training as a strategic weapon. They should train all their people in the basic concepts of quality management tied closely to job functions and individual needs.
-CEO, Modi Xerox

The customer should always to be kept in view. He is not buying your product as a monument; it has to serve his purpose. So, quality is what is perfect from the point of view of the customer. Suitable training is a must to upkeep quality, which customer expects us to give.

The training may be

- in plant training
- overseas training
- supervisory development training
- stress management
- risk management
- quality controls
- safety management
- hospitality management
- cost consciousness
- computer software programming
- modern natural internet technology training
- environment management
- yoga
- customer relations management
- housekeeping training
- Labor management laws and cordial relations training etc.

All these training lead to the road of success in an organization.

Only when a man is trained can he blossom!

Ranbaxy always speak high about the consequences of good training. They stress that worker's should be educated continuously on Corporate goals.

Thermax gave training in such a way that every employee learns to use the ANAARO road map, a methodology, to improve processes. The road map was prepared by a Michigan Consultancy.

When Deepak Parekh, CEO HDFC, was asked how efficiency & quality in service was built he said "It was learning by doing".

In ABB, training technique is somewhat different.

They plan every team member's job and his training – for the year ahead.

Training given to senior members to counsel employees in team functioning.

"We have made a beginning in driving home the point that if an individual wins, the company does not necessarily wins. But if a team wins, the individual also wins. - K.N. Shenoy, CEO, ABB

In IFB industries, each month, the quality review meeting goes thro' all the processes and discusses how they can be improved.

Likewise, true head of each department has to identify the training needs of his people.

"There are some who need training to perform even better, while others need it to keep up with the rest" - G.P. Chawla , G.M. IFB

Departmental requirements go via the Quality Systems' Chief to the management representative, who is formally responsible for training. In fact, in IFB's quality manual, which lists every senior manager's quality responsibility, there is only one that appears in every list: Identification of departmental training needs!

That is why IFBs quality strategy could be called the people product process trinity.

Communication Processes

No organization should be bogged down by operational problems, but should plan far ahead. The key is in installing a good communication system that is in tune with the needs of a growing organization. It is a system that respects information as a resource and helps you utilize it to the fullest extent.

"There are no bad workers, only bad managers. If they can't provide good communication leadership during recession, then there is something wrong with them – and not with workers - said Swraj Paul, owner of multi crore CAPARO groups of Industries, in one of his bold interview to Business Today.

A good communication with all managers helped him to find out how well managers are performing or not performing. He advised and guided his sons Ambar Paul and Anzag Paul in similar style.

Swraj Paul rates his manager by the degree of dependence on the head office for decisions. He expected his managers to have close contact with workers with good communication skills to extract work to reach the target.

Good communication is the life and blood of all success.

In the book "The power of ethical persuasion" Tom Rusk a leading management consultant in Chicago writes "Here's a unique step by step guide for that unpopular manager – who forces all those unpleasant management decisions down employee's throats to re vamp his corporate image".

Tom Rusk says that trick is to communicate in a manner, which makes it evident that you can see the other person's point of view.

The solution lies in ethical persuasion, where you try to understand the reasons behind the other person's opposition and then explain just why those terms are unfounded.

Communication turns ugly within an organization because of two unwritten laws.

Only bosses are allowed to get angry and no one else.

"Break both" says Rusk, "to ensure that sympathetic understanding becomes the key note of all communication".

Communication skills and the relationship that you develop with other employees in your organization help you bridge the gap between the goals that you set for yourself and the outcome that you achieve.

Peter Druckers says every decision has two elements.

- ideally what you would like to do and

- what you are actually able to do

If you want to do more of the former, consider becoming an expert in Communication skills:

In Wipro, communications from bottom line are highly regarded for major decisions. Even if he is a new comer have an ear for his works and have an eye on his fresh spirit, says it's CEO.

Job Rotation:

Job rotation enriches knowledge.

Young aspirants should be rotated and utilized fully.

Any emergency will require the assistance of anybody and nobody should say "That's not my job, that's none of my business and I know nothing about those processes. Those machines & techniques are new to me".

No.

Nobody should deny handling any project or assignment with ease. A good job rotation builds confidence and makes him a jack of all trades.

As Swraj Paul said, "I give job rotation to me too. I drive my own car when my driver is absent. Because I know with that skill I am able to save time, money at times of necessity".

Motorola Six Sigma Process for TQM is outstanding and exemplary.

The key stone to Motorola business philosophy is quality.

Quality as process is well captured in their Six Sigma Program.

And quality as people whose mandate is to manage the processes that lead to quality.

It's people, who must be capable of meeting the diverse demands that quality makes. On the one hand, conformity with stringent procedures and systems requires a disciplined mind-set and approach.

On the other hand, innovation and entrepreneurial instinct are the key ingredients for providing high quality products and services to customers.

And have two extremities must be straddled by people, who in addition must powers high degree of technical competence.

For TQM, Motorola implements as follows:

- Employees are empowered to take decisions. They are made self driven.

- Creating culture to see that jobs are made more challenging.

- Right people are selected.

- Hire for attitude and train for skill is their strategy.

- Selection is based on psyche match – whether recurred is culturally compatible with the organizations philosophy of operating without constant reference to instructions.

- Incentives to team based performance.

- 40 hrs training per annum is mandatory for all employees.

- Make employees educated thro' Motorola University.

- To leverage the knowledge assets of the individuals.

"My vision is to make Motorola India, a resource base of technical and managerial talent for the rest of the Corporation in the next millennium.

With the quality of the people we attract, I have no doubt we will soon achieve this mission. - Amit Sharma, CEO, Motorola India.

HRD Quotable Quotes

The HRD instruments systems play a vital role in an organization for fulfillment of goals.

They are to be implemented with utmost care to serve the purpose.

Only quality people make quality Products. That's why we have
Invested significantly in HRD – ensuring tomorrows leadership and maximizing today's diverse wealth of talent. - CEO, Indian Dye Stuff, Industries Limited

Our HRD systems are something that stay behind and can be used by anybody irrespective of who comes and who goes. - CEO. Modi Xerox

Educate workers continuously on corporate goals. HRD does the magic at all situations for productivity. -CEO Ranbaxy.

Strange India

https://www.amazon.co.uk/dp/B07S73LCTK

Waves of Wit on the Sea of Satire: Fun Butter Jam!!

https://www.amazon.co.uk/dp/B07XF5DT72

Kohlinoor of India: Winner Virat Kohli

https://www.amazon.co.uk/dp/B07SKNRVCT

Never Forgotten Naradar Srinivasa Rao: Most Enterprising Journalist

https://www.amazon.co.uk/dp/B07NLFY73C

How to Manage Funds in an Organization?

https://www.amazon.co.uk/dp/B00Z0Q8IF8

Wonders of Nano Technology

https://www.amazon.co.uk/dp/B07D3ZP7MC

How to become a Leader?

https://www.amazon.com/dp/B08BF4HCVX

What are the Best HRD Tactics?

https://www.amazon.co.uk/dp/B07HZ7JK18

Solar Energy Plans in Tamilnadu

https://www.amazon.co.uk/dp/B01G44ZL4K

How to Forecast Manpower Needs in an Organization: You Have The Skill!

https://www.amazon.co.uk/dp/B0111GBZKK

Infrastructure in India

https://www.amazon.co.uk/dp/B0163777RW

Accountant's Role in an Organization: A book for Accountants

https://www.amazon.co.uk/dp/B00YYHDHU0

Inland Waterways and Hydro Power in India

https://www.amazon.co.uk/dp/B015NEZMXW

Strategies in an Organization

https://www.amazon.co.uk/dp/B015AV1ZWU

Conflict Management Styles and Collective Bargaining

https://www.amazon.co.uk/dp/B00Z3B9GTW

Quiz and General Knowledge

https://www.amazon.co.uk/dp/B01N4M99S7

In Search of Paradise and Peace

https://www.amazon.co.uk/dp/B07C7F3XKM

Graphene -The God of Nano Technology

https://www.amazon.co.uk/dp/B07561LWTT

You Can Gain Power and Authority

https://www.amazon.co.uk/dp/B00YWY9QR8

HRD Systems and Management by Objectives

https://www.amazon.co.uk/dp/B016UC9UKC

International Conferences on Nanotechnology in India

https://www.amazon.co.uk/dp/B07BP8YLJZ

Holy Madhwa Saints: Get Divine Pleasure by Reading

https://www.amazon.co.uk/dp/B010WNBYU4

Trade Shows in India and Participants

https://www.amazon.co.uk/dp/B016PV1KS8

Collaboration and Intervention Techniques

https://www.amazon.co.uk/dp/B0110DLE8C

How to Plan Career and Quality Discipline in an Organization? Plan for Prosperity

https://www.amazon.co.uk/dp/B011GXOXIE

How to Become a Professional Manager? For You It Is Possible!

https://www.amazon.co.uk/dp/B011G4T6BM

Process of Planning and Control

https://www.amazon.co.uk/dp/B010ZHIBJE

How to Speak Skillfully?

https://www.amazon.com/dp/B08BJ8PCKT

How to Supervise Efficiently?

https://www.amazon.com/dp/B08BNFYSPQ- e book
https://www.amazon.com/dp/B08BR8YYG6?ref_=pe_
3052080_397514860

How to Develop Systems for Profit?

https://www.amazon.com/dp/B08BYVL2P9

Nanotechnology Research in India

https://www.amazon.com/dp/B08BZDFVR8

Click to see my e books published by amazon

http://www.amazon.com/s/ref=la_B01G3JTQ92_B01G3JTQ92_sr?rh=i%3Abooks&field-author=Chakrapani+Srinivasa&sort=relevance&ie=UTF8

A good HRD manager gives success and turnaround to an organization

www.ingramcontent.com/pod-product-compliance
Lightning Source LLC
Chambersburg PA
CBHW030545220526

45463CB00007B/2991